INSECTS &
SPIDERS

DANGEROUS
INSECTS & SPIDERS

Chris McNab

GARETH**STEVENS**
GS
PUBLISHING
A Member of the WRC Media Family of Companies

Please visit our Web site at: **www.garethstevens.com**
For a free color catalog describing Gareth Stevens Publishing's
list of high-quality books and multimedia programs,
call 1-800-542-2595 (USA) or 1-800-387-3178 (Canada).
Gareth Stevens Publishing's fax: (414) 332-3567.

Library of Congress Cataloging-in-Publication Data

McNab, Chris.
    Dangerous insects & spiders / Chris McNab.
       p. cm. — (Nature's monsters. Insects & spiders)
    Includes bibliographical references and index.
    ISBN-10: 0-8368-6848-X — ISBN-13: 978-0-8368-6848-7 (lib. bdg.)
    1. Insects—Juvenile literature. 2. Spiders—Juvenile literature. 3. Insect pests—Juvenile
literature. 4. Dangerous animals–Juvenile literature. I. Title: Dangerous insects and spiders.
II. Title. III. Series.
QL467.2.M375   2006
595.7165—dc22   2006042358

This North American edition first published in 2007 by
Gareth Stevens Publishing
A Member of the WRC Media Family of Companies
330 West Olive Street, Suite 100
Milwaukee, WI 53212 USA

Original edition and illustrations copyright © 2006 by International Masters Publishers AB.
Produced by Amber Books Ltd., Bradley's Close, 74–77 White Lion Street, London N1 9PF, U.K.

Project editor: Michael Spilling
Design: Joe Conneally

Gareth Stevens editorial direction: Valerie J. Weber
Gareth Stevens editor: Leifa Butrick
Gareth Stevens art direction: Tammy West
Gareth Stevens production: Jessica Morris

Printed in the United States of America

1 2 3 4 5 6 7 8 9 10 09 08 07 06

Contents

Continents of the World

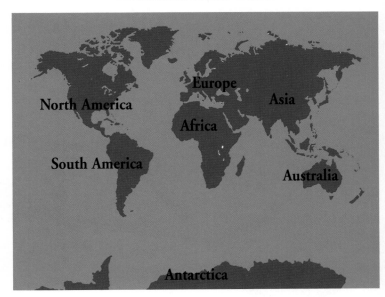

The world is divided into seven continents — North America, South America, Europe, Africa, Asia, Australia, and Antarctica. On the following pages, the area where each animal lives is shown in red, while all land is shown in green.

Words that appear in the glossary are printed in **boldface** type the first time they occur in the text.

Florida Walking Stick

The body looks like a stick, so the insect has excellent **camouflage** among branches.

It uses its outer jaws — known as **mandibles** — to cut up food. Its inner jaws chew up the food for swallowing.

The walking stick has claws on the end of each leg that give it a strong grip on branches.

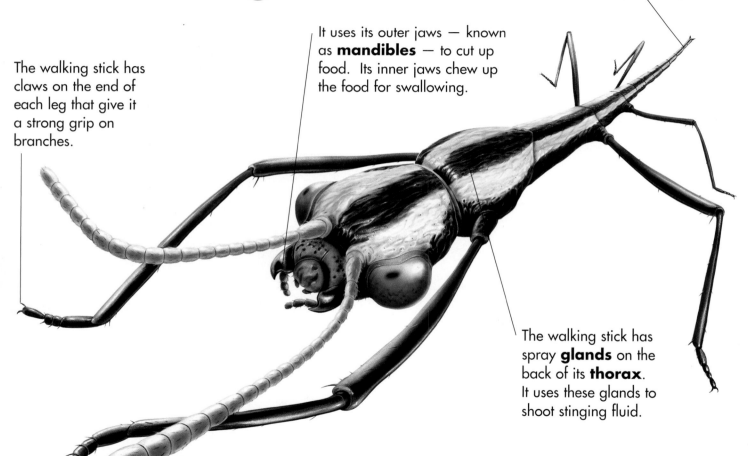

The walking stick has spray **glands** on the back of its **thorax**. It uses these glands to shoot stinging fluid.

The glands on the back of a Florida walking stick can spray out jets of stinging fluid for 27 inches (68 centimeters). Anyone hit in the eyes by this spray feels terrible pain and will not be able to see well for days.

1 A Florida jay bird spots a walking stick trying to hide in some tree branches. The jay moves in for the kill. As the bird opens its bill, the walking stick hits it in the face with two blasts of stinging fluid from its spray glands.

Actual Size

Did You Know?

If a **predator** grabs a stick insect's leg, the leg drops off so the insect can escape. A young stick insect can grow another leg in its place, but an adult will have to live with five instead of six legs.

2 The spray covers the bird's eyes and goes down its nose and throat. The bird flies away in pain, and the walking stick is safe.

Where in the World

The Florida walking stick lives in **tropical** territories surrounding the Gulf of Mexico. It lives in trees and shrubs, and it comes out at night to eat leaves.

Malarial Mosquito

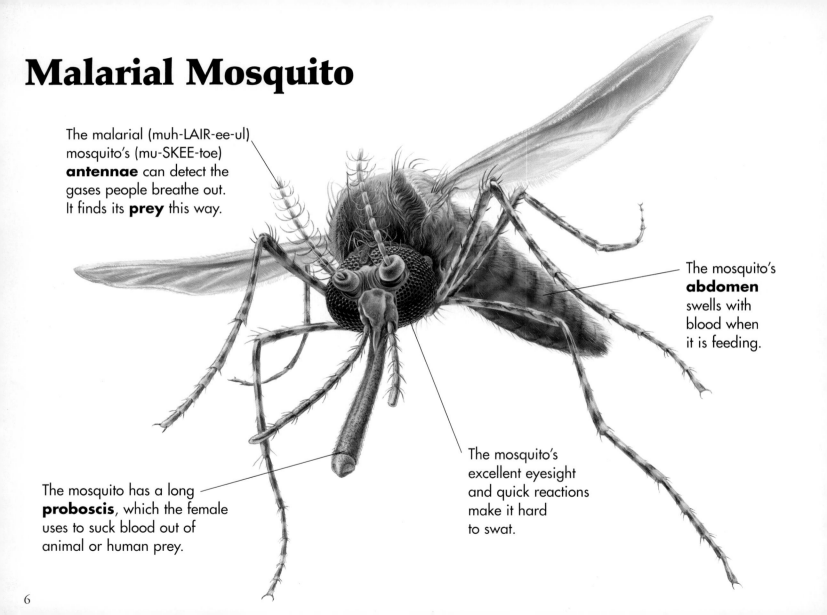

The malarial (muh-LAIR-ee-ul) mosquito's (mu-SKEE-toe) **antennae** can detect the gases people breathe out. It finds its **prey** this way.

The mosquito's **abdomen** swells with blood when it is feeding.

The mosquito has a long **proboscis**, which the female uses to suck blood out of animal or human prey.

The mosquito's excellent eyesight and quick reactions make it hard to swat.

Female mosquitoes produce thousands of young each year. A female lays its eggs on water. It may choose puddles of rainwater, lakes, or rivers.

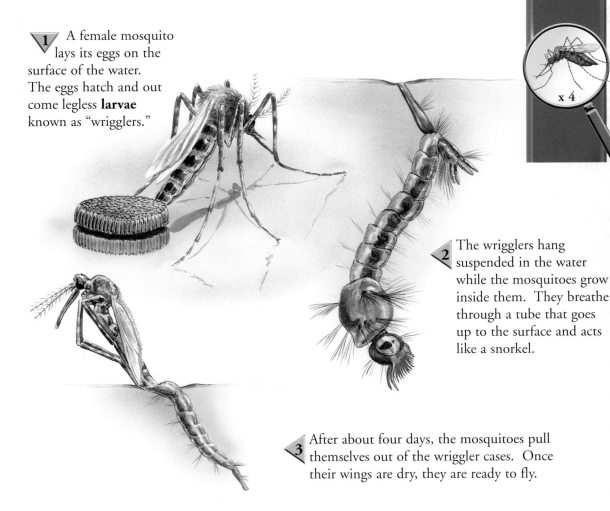

1 A female mosquito lays its eggs on the surface of the water. The eggs hatch and out come legless **larvae** known as "wrigglers."

2 The wrigglers hang suspended in the water while the mosquitoes grow inside them. They breathe through a tube that goes up to the surface and acts like a snorkel.

3 After about four days, the mosquitoes pull themselves out of the wriggler cases. Once their wings are dry, they are ready to fly.

Did You Know?

In tropical parts of the world, infected female mosquitoes pass a **lethal** disease called **malaria** to humans. Every year, up to two million people die of malaria.

Where in the World

Mosquitoes live almost everywhere in the world, apart from **polar regions**. Malarial mosquitoes, however, live in the tropical parts of Asia, Africa, and South America.

Killer Bee

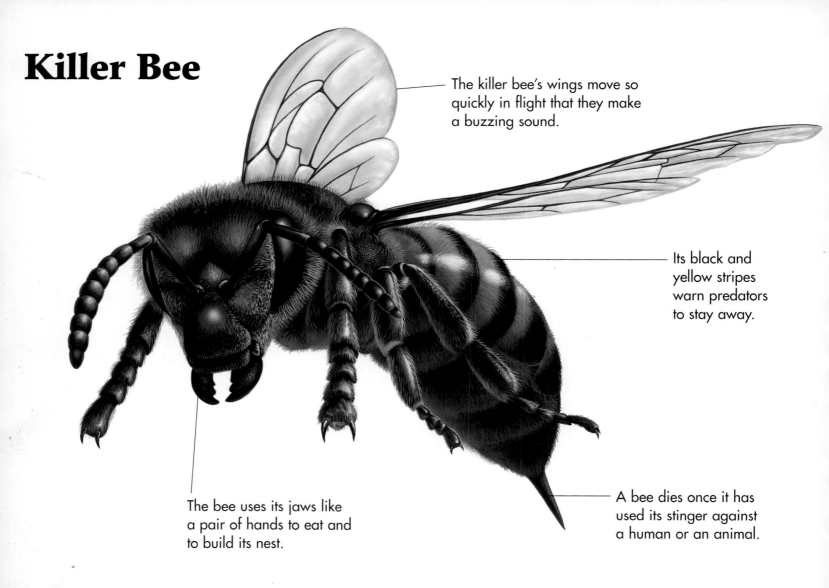

The killer bee's wings move so quickly in flight that they make a buzzing sound.

Its black and yellow stripes warn predators to stay away.

The bee uses its jaws like a pair of hands to eat and to build its nest.

A bee dies once it has used its stinger against a human or an animal.

When disturbed, killer bees will attack anything that crosses their path. A bee's stinger is made up of two spikes. The spikes have **barbs** on them, which catch onto skin when the bee stings. When the bee moves away, the stinger and its **venom sac** are dragged out of the bee's body, and it dies.

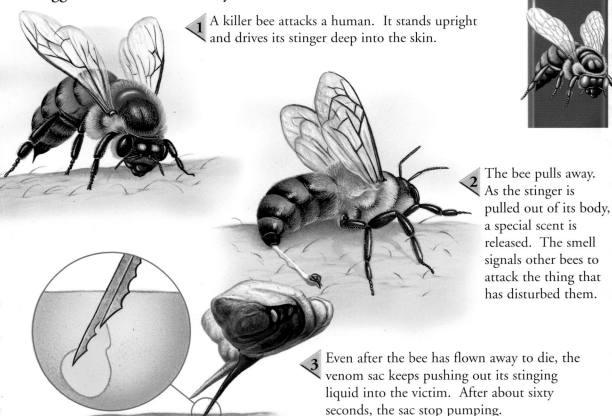

1 A killer bee attacks a human. It stands upright and drives its stinger deep into the skin.

2 The bee pulls away. As the stinger is pulled out of its body, a special scent is released. The smell signals other bees to attack the thing that has disturbed them.

3 Even after the bee has flown away to die, the venom sac keeps pushing out its stinging liquid into the victim. After about sixty seconds, the sac stop pumping.

Actual Size

Bird-Eating Spider

A bird-eating spider has three pairs of **spinnerets**. It uses these to spin silk nests.

Although the bird-eating spider has eight eyes, its eyesight is very poor. It relies on its strong sense of touch and smell to catch prey.

The spider has two hollow **fangs** that it uses to inject venom into its prey.

The spider uses its **pedipalps** like arms to sense objects and to grab its prey before biting it.

Bird-eating spiders mainly eat insects, lizards, frogs, and bats. They also eat baby birds, which are helpless against the spider's attack.

Bird-eating spiders can be up to 6 inches (15 cm) wide from the end of one leg to another. Some relatives of the bird-eating spider are much larger, measuring 12 inches (30 cm) from the tip of one leg to the other.

1

A bird-eating spider finds a nest of chicks high in the branches of a tree. It crawls into the middle of the nest and chooses one of the chicks. Gripping the chick with its **pedipalps**, the spider sinks its fangs into the bird's back, killing it with its lethal **venom**.

2 To eat the chick, the spider **injects** powerful **digestive juices** into the bird's body. The juices turn the bird's insides into liquid, and the spider then sucks up the **liquefied** flesh to eat.

Where in the World

Bird-eating spiders live in northern South America. Their preferred **habitat** is a tropical **rain forest**. Here, they find plenty of food and water and many plants to live among.

Cockroach

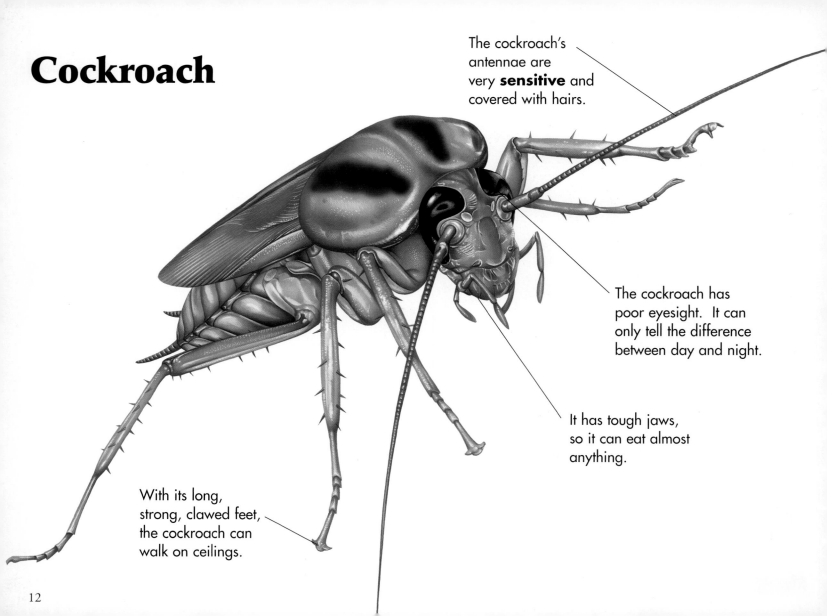

The cockroach's antennae are very **sensitive** and covered with hairs.

The cockroach has poor eyesight. It can only tell the difference between day and night.

It has tough jaws, so it can eat almost anything.

With its long, strong, clawed feet, the cockroach can walk on ceilings.

Cockroaches are difficult to kill. They have sensitive hairs that warn them of danger approaching. They are born survivors and can exist almost anywhere. Unfortunately, cockroaches spread disease.

Actual Size

Did You Know?

Cockroaches have lived on Earth for more than 300 million years. A single cockroach can produce 7 million new adults in one year.

Cockroaches were probably the first animals in space, because they are often found on spacecraft.

1 During the night, these cockroaches have found a dead rat. They begin eating the body, and soon their mouths, bodies, and legs are covered in **bacteria** from the rat.

2 Later, the cockroaches pick up a scent and go to the kitchen. They squeeze under even the tiniest gap in the door.

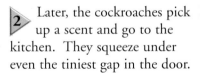

3 The cockroaches are now in a restaurant kitchen. They scramble onto a table and find a plate of food. They begin munching on it, and when the waiter comes to pick up the plate, they run away.

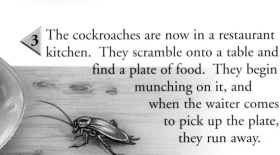

Where in the World

Cockroaches can be found all around the world, mainly close to humans. They like warm, damp buildings but can live in ships and airplanes.

13

Mexican Red-Knee Tarantula

A tough outer shell protects the Mexican red-knee tarantula's (tuh-RAN-chew-luh) head and upper body from harm.

The "legs" on either side of the tarantula's jaws are, in fact, feelers. It uses these feelers to explore the ground in front of it.

The tarantula's legs are covered with thick hairs that pick up smells and **vibrations**.

The tarantula is a dangerous type of spider. Its jaws contain a pair of huge, needle-sharp fangs. It uses these fangs to inject venom into its prey.

A Mexican red-knee tarantula feeds on insects, small lizards, and **rodents**. It lies in wait in its **burrow**, and attacks any prey that comes too close to the entrance.

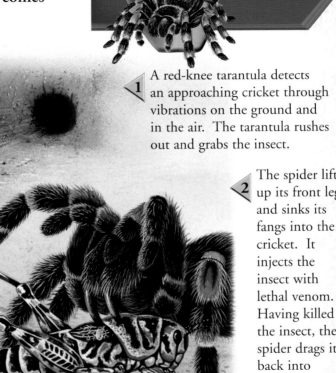

1 A red-knee tarantula detects an approaching cricket through vibrations on the ground and in the air. The tarantula rushes out and grabs the insect.

2 The spider lifts up its front legs and sinks its fangs into the cricket. It injects the insect with lethal venom. Having killed the insect, the spider drags it back into its **lair**.

3 There, the spider injects digestive juices into the insect's body, which turn the insect's insides into liquid. The spider then sucks up the flesh through its mouth.

Did You Know?

Tarantulas look terrifying, but their bites rarely kill healthy human beings. If threatened, however, they flick out clouds of hairs from their abdomens. These hairs hurt people's eyes and affect their breathing.

Where in the World

Mexican red-knee tarantulas live in the deserts of northwestern and central Mexico. Unfortunately, they are an endangered animal because people have taken too many as pets.

15

Old World Scorpion

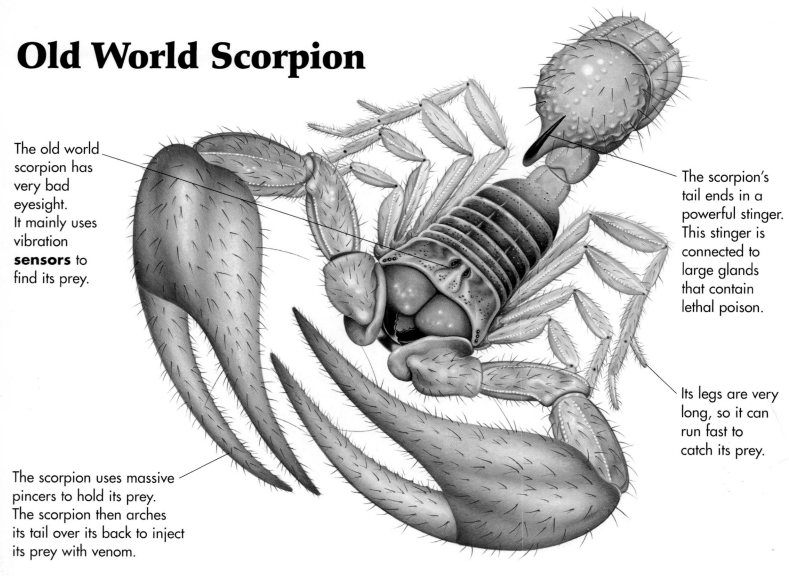

The old world scorpion has very bad eyesight. It mainly uses vibration **sensors** to find its prey.

The scorpion's tail ends in a powerful stinger. This stinger is connected to large glands that contain lethal poison.

Its legs are very long, so it can run fast to catch its prey.

The scorpion uses massive pincers to hold its prey. The scorpion then arches its tail over its back to inject its prey with venom.

16

Old world scorpions will not attack human beings for no reason. Usually, they sting people only after they are accidentally stepped on or cornered.

1 A family in southern Spain wanders barefoot along a beautiful beach. They do not see a scorpion basking in the sun.

2 The little boy steps on the scorpion. Like lightning, it stabs the boy's foot with its stinger. The boy screams in pain, then falls onto the sand. He is soon **paralyzed**. He will die if his parents do not get him to a doctor quickly.

Size

Where in the World

Old world scorpions cover a wide area, including southern Europe, North Africa, and the Middle East. The kinds found in North Africa and the Middle East are the most dangerous.

Bark Scorpion

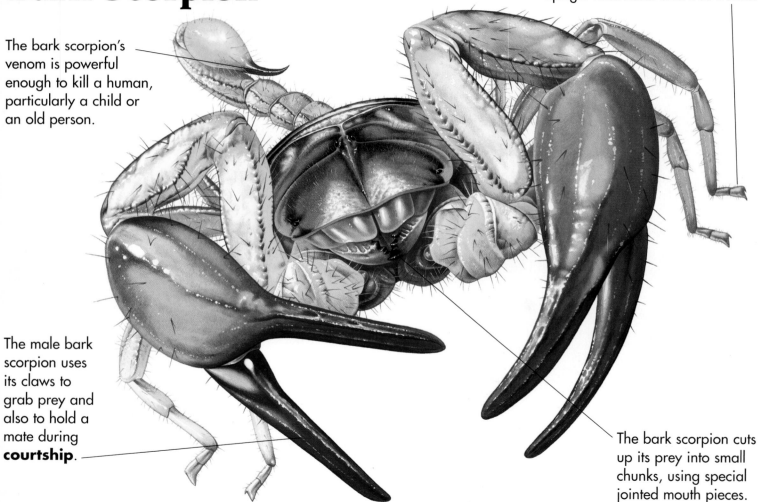

The bark scorpion's venom is powerful enough to kill a human, particularly a child or an old person.

The bark scorpion has sharp claws on its feet that allow it to climb upright rock faces and tree trunks.

The male bark scorpion uses its claws to grab prey and also to hold a mate during **courtship**.

The bark scorpion cuts up its prey into small chunks, using special jointed mouth pieces.

18

Bark scorpions like to shelter from the sun during daylight. Being good climbers, they often climb up into trees and hide themselves under branches or pieces of loose bark.

1 In the hot Arizona desert, a cowboy stops for a rest. He does not know that a bark scorpion is sitting on the branch just above his head.

2 The cowboy pulls himself to his feet using the branch and touches the scorpion. The scorpion stings him with its tail. People who have been stung by a bark scorpion often feel sick and numb and have blurred vision and breathing difficulties. If he does not get an **antivenom** in a hospital quickly, he could die.

Size

Where in the World

Bark scorpions are found from the southern United States through to the northern parts of South America and on the Caribbean islands. They like warm, dry habitats.

Emperor Scorpion

Its arms are covered with long hairs. These hairs can feel vibrations in the air and the direction they come from.

A tough outer shell known as an **exoskeleton** protects the emperor scorpion's body.

The emperor scorpion can grow up to 8 inches (20 cm) long.

The scorpion uses its huge claws for fighting, for digging burrows, and for holding prey.

Scorpions find moving prey by using the sensitive hairs on their arms to pick up vibrations in the air. They also pick up vibrations on the ground through feathery hairs on the undersides of their bodies.

1 It is night, and an emperor scorpion is hiding beneath a pile of leaves. It senses the vibrations of a cricket moving past. The scorpion rushes out and grabs the cricket in its strong claws.

Size

2 Adult emperor scorpions kill their prey using their claws. The scorpion cuts up the cricket with its jaws and uses chemicals from its stomach to turn the cricket's flesh into soupy liquid for eating.

Where in the World

The emperor scorpion lives in the western parts of Africa, from Senegal to the Congo. It prefers to live in hot and damp tropical rain forests, but it is also found in dry African grasslands.

Desert Locust

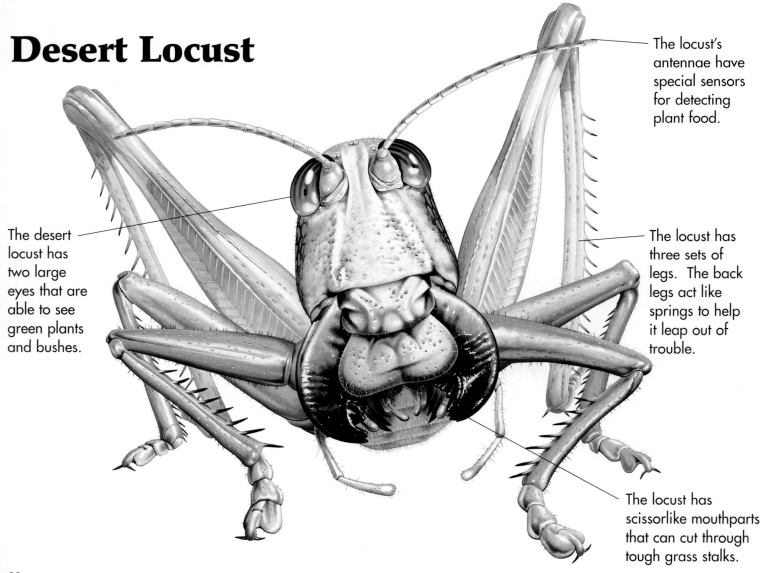

The locust's antennae have special sensors for detecting plant food.

The desert locust has two large eyes that are able to see green plants and bushes.

The locust has three sets of legs. The back legs act like springs to help it leap out of trouble.

The locust has scissorlike mouthparts that can cut through tough grass stalks.

Locust swarms feed on stalks, flowers, leaves, fruit, and almost any type of crop. They are one of the most dangerous threats to farmers in poor countries.

1 In Africa, a farmer stands helpless as an enormous swarm of locusts slashes through his crop of millet grain. It will take only a few hours for the insects to eat the whole field.

Size

2 Locust swarms are very active after rainfall. The fresh vegetation that follows rainfall encourages the locusts to **breed** quickly. They breed so fast that the swarm is forced to move off to find fresh crops to feed their young.

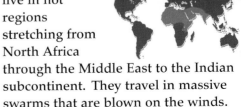

European Hornet

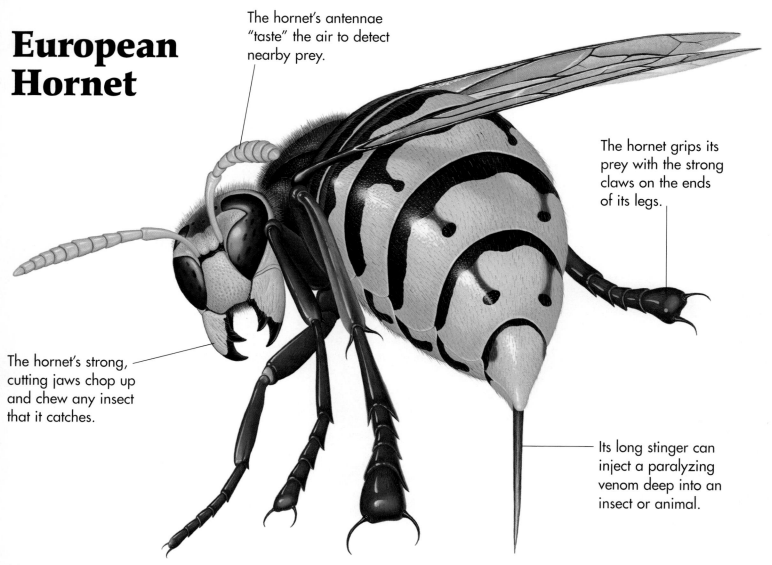

The hornet's antennae "taste" the air to detect nearby prey.

The hornet grips its prey with the strong claws on the ends of its legs.

The hornet's strong, cutting jaws chop up and chew any insect that it catches.

Its long stinger can inject a paralyzing venom deep into an insect or animal.

24

Hornets will attack anyone that comes too close to their nests. Worker hornets hunt constantly, killing insects to feed to their growing larvae.

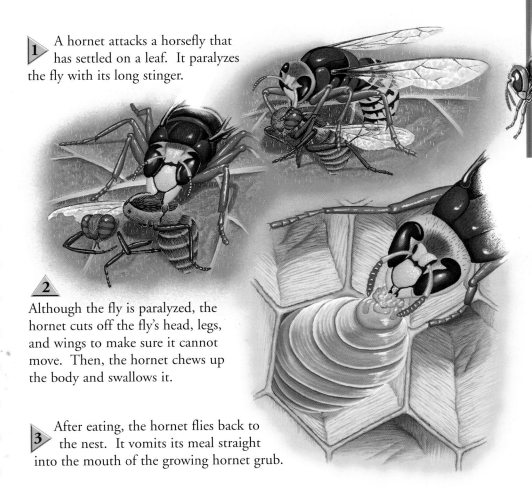

1 A hornet attacks a horsefly that has settled on a leaf. It paralyzes the fly with its long stinger.

2 Although the fly is paralyzed, the hornet cuts off the fly's head, legs, and wings to make sure it cannot move. Then, the hornet chews up the body and swallows it.

3 After eating, the hornet flies back to the nest. It vomits its meal straight into the mouth of the growing hornet grub.

Actual Size

Where in the World

European hornets are found in much of the world. In the United States, they are found all along the East Coast and west to Louisiana and the Dakotas. They also live in Europe, Asia, Canada, and Madagascar.

25

Plague Flea

The **plague** flea has small eyes that can do little more than tell the difference between day and night. The flea uses scent and sound to find its prey.

A tough outer covering protects the plague flea's body from animals' nails, claws, and teeth.

The plague flea is covered with spiny hairs. These hairs catch on animal hair or fur to enable the flea to hang on to its **host**.

The flea's sharp mouthparts can cut through the most leathery animal skin.

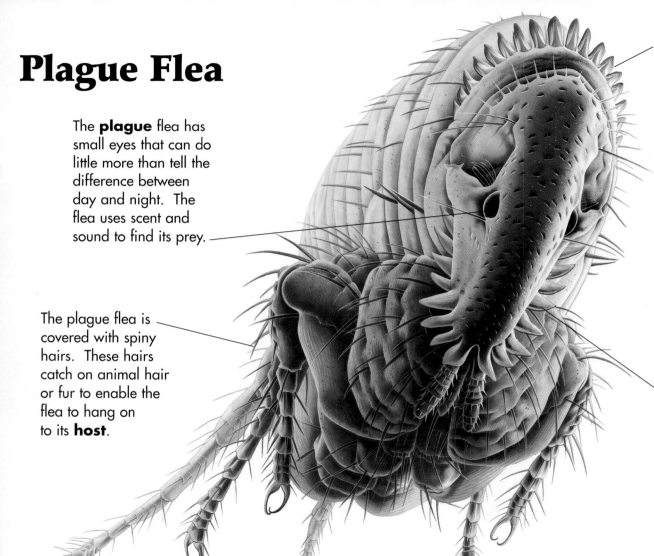

Fleas drink animal blood, leaping from host to host using their amazing jumping powers. They pass on plague bacteria when they bite through an animal's skin.

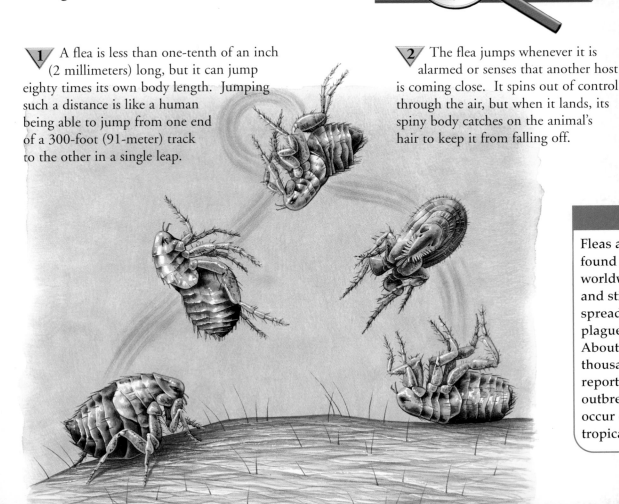

1 A flea is less than one-tenth of an inch (2 millimeters) long, but it can jump eighty times its own body length. Jumping such a distance is like a human being able to jump from one end of a 300-foot (91-meter) track to the other in a single leap.

2 The flea jumps whenever it is alarmed or senses that another host is coming close. It spins out of control through the air, but when it lands, its spiny body catches on the animal's hair to keep it from falling off.

Elegant Grasshopper

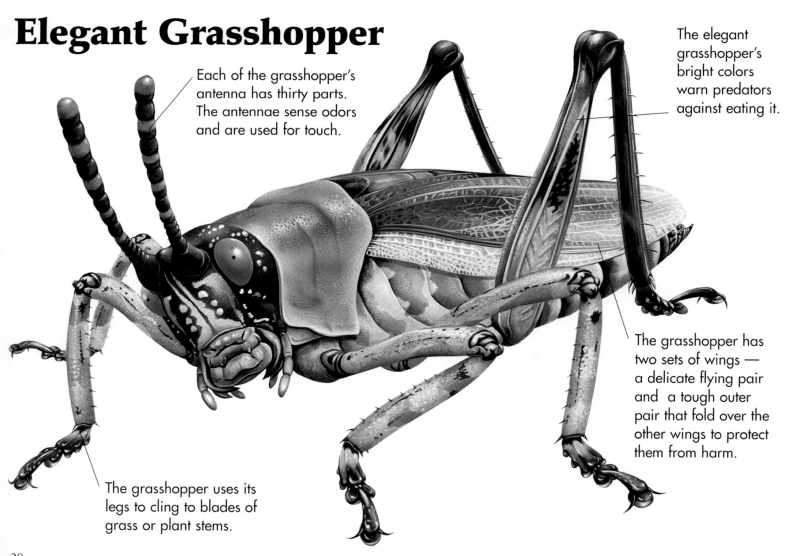

Each of the grasshopper's antenna has thirty parts. The antennae sense odors and are used for touch.

The elegant grasshopper's bright colors warn predators against eating it.

The grasshopper has two sets of wings — a delicate flying pair and a tough outer pair that fold over the other wings to protect them from harm.

The grasshopper uses its legs to cling to blades of grass or plant stems.

Elegant grasshoppers make themselves poisonous by eating **toxic** plants, such as the Siam weed. If a predator eats a poisonous grasshopper. The animal will feel very sick. It will learn not to eat elegant grasshoppers again.

Actual Size

1 A young jackal is out hunting for food with its mother. It sees an elegant grasshopper on a branch. In spite of the bright colors the jackal eats the grasshopper down quickly.

2 The poisons in the grasshopper quickly make the jackal feel sick. The jackal vomits everything in its stomach. Although the poison has done no permanent damage, the jackal has learned its lesson.

Where in the World

Elegant grasshoppers are found in most of Africa south of the Sahara Desert. They live in a variety of habitats, including grasslands, rain forests, forests, farmlands, and gardens. They can destroy many crops.

Glossary

abdomen — the lower section of an insect's body

antennae — a pair of long feelers on an insect's head

antivenom — a chemical that stops a poison from working

bacteria — tiny living things that can cause illness

barbs — small, sharp pointed objects pointing backward, like arrows or fishhooks

breed — to make baby animals

burrow — hole made in the ground by an animal for shelter and protection

camouflage — the pattern on an animal's skin that helps hide it

courtship — the process of performing certain actions to attract a breeding partner

digestive juices — liquids produced in the body that help break down food so that the body can use it for energy

exoskeleton — a tough skeleton on the outside of an animal's body

fangs — long teeth, often containing poison

glands — parts of the body that make special chemicals needed for the body to work properly

habitat — a place where an animal or plant lives

host — an animal that another animal lives upon

injects — forces fluid or poison into a body

lair — an animal's resting or sleeping place

larvae — young, developing insects

lethal — able to kill

liquefied — turned into liquid

malaria — a disease spread by the female mosquito

mandibles — a pair of pincerlike jaws used by insects to cut up food

paralyzed — unable to move

pedipalps — a pair of feelers between a spider's front legs

plague — a serious disease carried by rodents and spread to humans and other animals by fleas

polar regions — the icy lands of the Arctic and Antarctic

predator — animal that hunts, kills, and eats other animals

prey — an animal hunted and killed for food

proboscis — a long tubelike nose used by an insect for feeding; also a long snout

rain forest — thick forest or jungle where lots of rain falls

rodents — a group of small, furry animals that includes rats, hamsters, and mice

sac — a pouch within an animal or plant, often containing fluid

sensitive — easily affected by touch, sight, smell, and sound

sensors — things that receive a signal and respond to it

spinnerets — the part of a spider's body that makes silk

swarms — large numbers of insects together

thorax — the middle part of an insect between the head and the abdomen

toxic — poisonous

tropical — referring to the hottest parts of the world, with lush plant life

venom — a poison made by an animal

vibrations — tiny motions caused by sounds or movements

For More Information

Books

Funnel Web Spiders. Dangerous Spiders (series).
   Eric Ethan (Gareth Stevens)

Killer Bees. Dangerous Creatures (series).
   Marcia Hinds (Capstone Press)

Killer Bees. Dillon Remarkable Animals Book (series).
   Kathleen Davis (Dillon)

Locusts. Gross Bugs (series). Jonathan Kravetz
   (PowerKids Press)

Scorpions: The Sneaky Stingers. Animals in Order (series).
   Allison Lassieur (Franklin Watts)

Tarantulas. Dangerous Spiders (series). Eric Ethan
   (Gareth Stevens)

Walking Stick. Bug Books (series). Monica Harris
   (Heinemann Library)

Youch!: Real-life Monsters Up Close. Trevor Day
   (Simon & Schuster)

Web Sites

Anatomy of a Hive
www.pbs.org/wgbh/nova/bees/hive.html

Australia Museum Online
www.amonline.net.au/spiders/

Classroom Clipart
classroomclipart.com/Animals/Insects

Enchanted Learning
www.enchantedlearning.com/themes/spiders.shtml

Insecta Inspecta World
www.insecta-inspecta.com

Spider Identification Chart
www.termite.com/spider-identification.html

Wonderful World of Insects
www.earthlife.net/insects

Publisher's note to educators and parents: Our editors have carefully reviewed these Web sites to ensure that they are suitable for children. Many Web sites change frequently, however, and we cannot guarantee that a site's future contents will continue to meet our high standards of quality and educational value. Be advised that children should be closely supervised whenever they access the Internet.

Index